ATHLETES AGAINST
WAR

MUHAMMAD ALI, BILL WALTON, CARLOS DELGADO, AND MORE

by Elliott Smith

Published by Capstone Press, an imprint of Capstone.
1710 Roe Crest Drive, North Mankato, Minnesota 56003
capstonepub.com

Library of Congress Cataloging-in-Publication Data is available on the Library
of Congress website.
ISBN: 9781663965929 (hardcover)
ISBN: 9781666321203 (paperback)
ISBN: 9781666321210 (ebook pdf)

Summary: Activists take a stand. They speak out and demand change. From
legendary boxer Muhammad Ali to baseball star Carlos Delgado, readers discover
the pro athletes who have affected change by speaking out against war and its
impact on society.

Image Credits
Alamy: REUTERS/Larry Downing, 5, PA Images, 16; AP Images, 11, 17, Stuart
Ramson, 21; Getty Images: ANNALISA KRAFT/Staff, 4, Matthew Ashton -
EMPICS/Contributor, 19, NBAE/Andrew D. Bernstein/Contributor, 25, NCAA
Photos/Contributor, 10, Popperfoto/Contributor, 15, Rolls Press/Popperfoto,
13; Newscom: Chris Hatfield/Icon SMI, 28, Polaris/Stephen Shames, 9, Reuters/
Mike Segar, 23, TNS/Pioneer Press/Steve Sadin, 27, UPI/Alexis C. Glenn, 29;
Shutterstock: wow.subtropica, Cover; Sports Illustrated: Neil Leifer/Contributor, 7

Editorial Credits
Editor: Erika L. Shores; Designer: Heidi Thompson; Media Researcher: Jo Miller;
Production Specialist: Tori Abraham

Printed and bound in the USA. PO4608

TABLE OF CONTENTS

Words in BOLD appear in the glossary.

INTRODUCTION

War is rarely popular. People fear for the loss of lives. Homes, buildings, and cities can be destroyed. Activism is how people can spur change. **Activist** movements bring people together for a common cause. Anti-war movements can make government officials rethink military action.

Activists use protests and marches to get their voices heard. They put pressure on governments to end **conflicts**. Activists also work to keep wars from happening in the first place.

Protesters against the Gulf War carried signs as they marched through Washington, D.C., in 1991.

Activist athletes can make a major impact with simple actions. A raised fist, taking a knee, or wearing a shirt have had major impacts on sports and on the world. Because their words carry so much weight, some athletes do not risk speaking out. They are often told to "stick to sports." Other athletes choose to speak up. Their work has played a big part in changing minds. But sometimes, their actions cost them their careers.

Activist and former NBA player Etan Thomas spoke at the White House in 2009.

VIETNAM

The Vietnam War (1955–1975) was a long, difficult conflict. It also happened during a time when protests were used to spark change. At first, most people supported the war. But over time, public opinion changed. Toward the end, many people were strongly against it. This led to some of the earliest examples of activist athletes.

MUHAMMAD ALI

Boxing legend Muhammad Ali never worried about speaking his mind. He had opinions on every subject. It was his views on the war that were among his most **controversial**. In 1967, at the height of the war, Ali was **drafted** into the U.S. Army. He refused to be **inducted**. This action led to much public debate.

Muhammad Ali spoke to the media about his refusal to be drafted into the military in 1967.

Ali, a **Muslim**, said his religious beliefs would not allow him to fight in the war. He also famously noted that he had no problems with the Vietnamese people.

"Keep asking me, no matter how long," he once rhymed. "On the war in Vietnam, I sing this song. I ain't got no **quarrel** with the Vietcong."

The champion's views were met with strong reactions. Many people thought it was wrong for him to refuse to serve. He was banned from boxing. He spent nearly four years out of the sport. Instead of fighting, Ali became the most public face to stand against the war. He never let go of his anti-war beliefs.

FACT

Muhammad Ali won an Olympic gold medal in 1960. In 1964, he became the world heavyweight champion. Ali would become the first boxer to win the heavyweight championship three times.

During the war, Muhammad Ali traveled around the country speaking about his anti-war beliefs.

BILL WALTON

University of California, Los Angeles (UCLA) had one of the best college basketball teams in the 1960s and '70s. One of the (very) big reasons for their success was Bill Walton. The 6-foot-11 (211-centimeter) center was the team's biggest star. He was also a freethinker. He didn't go along with what other people believed. Walton did not support the war in Vietnam and took part in several protests at UCLA.

Bill Walton (32) during the championship game in March 1972

Bill Walton helped other protesters build a barricade around a UCLA building during a May 1972 protest.

In 1972, Walton took part in a huge protest on UCLA's grounds. Walton and the basketball team had just won the national championship. But he felt protesting the war was more important than celebrating the win. Walton was one of many students arrested during the protest. Walton's play on the court made him well known outside of UCLA. His arrest brought attention to the activism happening at schools across the country.

DAVE MEGGYESY

Dave Meggyesy made a name for himself as an NFL linebacker for the St. Louis Cardinals. But he was also well known for thinking outside the box. He took a stand against the war in several ways. He asked his teammates to sign a **petition**. It called for the U.S. to leave Vietnam. He also paid for a bus to take a group to Washington, D.C., for a peace march.

Meggyesy's biggest show of protest may have been his simplest. In the 1960s, NFL players held their helmets and looked at the flag during the national anthem. In 1968, Meggyesy started looking down at the ground. Many people were upset by his actions.

Meggyesy felt he wasn't getting a fair chance from teams because of his activism. He retired before the 1970 season. He became an activist and public speaker instead.

Dave Meggyesy helped send people to marches, such as this one in Washington, D.C., in November 1969.

IMPORTANT MESSAGE

During a 1972 game, University of Washington football players rose to action. The Huskies refused to come out on the field before the second half of the game. They wanted a statement they had written against the war to be read. While it was met with boos, the players' voices were heard, and they finished the game.

GLOBAL CONFLICTS

It's not just U.S. athletes who take a stand. Athletes from around the world have used activism to shine a light on issues. Many of these moments of activism have come during the Olympics. Using the global stage of sports to protest isn't always appreciated. But these athletes were willing to risk their popularity to make a statement.

VERA CASLAVSKA

Gymnast Vera Caslavska was one of the best in her sport. In the 1968 Olympics, Caslavska looked to add to her three gold medals. But she was doing so with a great deal of sadness. Just two months earlier, the Soviet Union had taken over her home country of Czechoslovakia. She had been forced to go into hiding before the Games.

Caslavska won the gold in the floor exercise. But she caused a stir during the medal ceremony. She refused to look at the Soviet flag or take part in the anthem.

Caslavska's actions led to her being forced out of the sport. She was even banned from work or travel. She would remain away from the sport until the end of **Communism** in 1989.

Vera Caslavska (left) received a shared gold medal for floor exercise in 1968.

WLADYSLAW KOZAKIEWICZ

Pole vaulter Wladyslaw Kozakiewicz was from the country of Poland. He was prepared for a difficult experience in the 1980 Moscow Olympics. Many countries, including the U.S., were **boycotting** the games. They were sitting out to protest the Soviet Union taking over Afghanistan. Poland was under Russian influence but not part of the Soviet Union.

Wladyslaw Kozakiewicz competing in the pole vault in the 1980 Olympics

Wladyslaw Kozakiewicz gestured to the crowd after his record-breaking jump.

The deck was stacked against Kozakiewicz in the event. The pro-Soviet crowd booed him. But Kozakiewicz fought through it and broke the world record. On his final jump, he got up and made a rude gesture toward the pro-Soviet crowd. Soviet officials were angry. They wanted to remove his medal. Kozakiewicz was forced to leave Poland and move to West Germany until the end of Communism. But he didn't regret his small act.

"I know what I did gave other people a lot of happiness, showing that," he said. "And I'm proud I showed them—let them see that you can resist, in your own way."

SASA CURCIC

Soccer player Sasa Curcic was known for his skills on the field. But one day in March 1999, his message to soccer fans was more heartfelt. During that time, the war in Yugoslavia was raging. The North Atlantic Treaty Organization (NATO) decided to step in. They bombed places in Yugoslavia.

Curcic, a Serbian, was playing for Crystal Palace FC in England at the time. His family was still in Yugoslavia. Before a match on March 28, Curcic took the field holding a simple sign that read "Stop NATO Bombing." Many fans were surprised. But they still cheered for Curcic. He would later protest outside government buildings in London. The bombing ended in June. Curcic's career ended shortly after that. It ended partly due to the stress the protest put on him.

Sasa Curcic protested against the bombing in his country.

Yugoslavia —
STOP
NATO
BOMBING

Committee for Peace in the Balkans

ANTHEM PROTESTS

The national anthem is almost always played before sporting events in the United States. Activists who use the anthem to get their message across may face a strong backlash. But there is no denying it makes a powerful statement.

TONI SMITH

During the Iraq War (2003–2011), Toni Smith took a stand. The Manhattanville College basketball player wanted to protest the war and **racism**. Before a game in 2003, she turned her back to the flag during the national anthem. She also bowed her head.

Her actions drew attention from news media across the country. Soon, the stands of Manhattanville's tiny gym were filled with people. Many of them were angry at her protest. But Smith stayed strong in her beliefs. Today, she continues her activism. She is an organizer for the New York Civil Liberties Union. It is a group that protects the rights of all people.

Toni Smith stood with her back to the flag before a game on February 23, 2003.

ONE GAME PROTEST

In 2003, shortly after Smith's protest, University of Virginia's Deidra Chatman turned her back to the flag. She was protesting the way the government dealt with other countries. Many people were upset by her actions too. Because of this, Chatman decided to again face forward during the anthem. She did not want the negative attention to affect her team.

CARLOS DELGADO

Carlos Delgado was a star for the Toronto Blue Jays baseball team. People knew him as a thoughtful and skilled player. During the 2004 season, Delgado's quiet protest made headlines around the world.

Many teams had begun playing the song "God Bless America" during the 7th inning stretch in 2001. Players would take off their caps and stand at attention. Delgado was upset with the U.S. involvement in wars in both Afghanistan and Iraq. He decided to stay in the dugout during the song.

Delgado's show of activism drew anger at first, even though Delgado didn't mean to cause a fuss. "I would say that when you do [something like this], you do it because you feel it is the right thing to do," he said. "Not necessarily because you expect a specific result." After a time, Delgado's quiet protest was accepted by the public.

FACT

In 2006, Delgado received the Roberto Clemente Award. It honors players who show outstanding sportsmanship by helping others, on and off the field. Pro baseball star Clemente died in a plane crash in 1972. He was helping bring supplies to earthquake victims.

Carlos Delgado played for the
Toronto Blue Jays from 1993
to 2004. He played for Florida
in 2005 before joining the
New York Mets until 2009.

OFF-COURT ACTIVISM

Activism can go beyond the sidelines. Some athletes prefer to use their voices off the court. They speak out to protest not only war but issues such as racism. Taking a stand outside of sports can give activists an even larger audience for their beliefs. It can also make them a bigger target for those who disagree with them.

CRAIG HODGES

The Chicago Bulls were a basketball **dynasty** in the 1990s. Of course, superstar Michael Jordan got all the headlines. But there were several other players who had key moments. Craig Hodges was one of them. The sharpshooting guard was one of the best 3-point shooters in the NBA. He was also a passionate activist.

During his time with the Chicago Bulls, Craig Hodges's 3-point shooting skills helped win two championships.

The Bulls traveled to the White House after winning the championship in 1991. Hodges was ready. He dressed in traditional African clothing. He also wrote a letter to then-President George H.W. Bush. It addressed racism and the ongoing Gulf War. Hodges was criticized in the media for his actions.

Less than a year later, Hodges was out of the NBA. He still believes he was pushed out. He has said certain people did not like his activism, including his letter to the president.

FACT

Hodges tried for several years to get back into the NBA. But no team would take him. He worked as an assistant coach for the L.A. Lakers before coaching his former high school team in Park Forest, Illinois.

Craig Hodges speaking about his activism
and how it cost him his NBA career.

ETAN THOMAS

Etan Thomas is an activist at heart. The former NBA star can express himself very well. As a published poet, Thomas used his words and actions to protest war.

Thomas spoke out loudly against the Iraq War. He gave a speech at a large anti-war rally in Washington, D.C., in 2005. He also held many interviews saying he was against the war. All this happened while he was playing for the Washington Wizards.

Etan Thomas played in the NBA from 2001 to 2011.

In 2008, Etan Thomas spoke at events for presidential candidate Barack Obama.

"I am totally against this war," he said at the time. "What's truly unpatriotic is misleading an entire nation into war under false **pretenses**."

Today, Thomas continues to support a number of causes. He serves as a mentor, or guide. He helps other athletes use their voices. They speak out and stand up for the things that matter to them.

GLOSSARY

activist (AK-tiv-ist)—a person who works for social or political change

boycott (BOY-kaht)—to refuse to take part in something as a way of making a protest

Communism (KAHM-yuh-ni-zuhm)—a way of running a country in which the government owns almost everything

conflict (KON-flict)—a struggle between people or countries that may be physical or be between differing ideas

controversial (kon-truh-VUR-shuhl)—causing disagreement or argument

draft (DRAFT)—to select young people to serve in the military

dynasty (DYE-nuh-stee)—a team that wins multiple championships over a period of several years

induct (in-DUHKT)—to take in as a member of military service

Muslim (MUHZ-luhm)—someone who follows the religion of Islam

petition (puh-TISH-uhn)—to make a formal request

pretense (PRE-tenss)—an act or appearance that looks real but is false

quarrel (KWOR-uhl)—a cause for disagreement

racism (RAY-siz-uhm)—the belief that one race is better than another race

READ MORE

Patterson, James, and Kwame Alexander. *Becoming Muhammad Ali*. New York: Little, Brown and Company, 2020.

Swift, Keilly. *How to Make a Better World*. New York: Dorling Kindersley, Inc., 2020.

We Are the Change: Words of Inspiration from Civil Rights Leaders. San Francisco: Chronicle Books, 2019.

INTERNET SITES

SI.com: The Activist Athlete
si.com/sportsperson/2020/12/06/sportsperson-2020-james-stewart-mahomes-osaka-duvernay-tardif

Teaching for Change: Athletes, Protest, and Patriotism
teachingforchange.org/athletes-protest-and-patriotism

INDEX

ABOUT THE AUTHOR

Elliott Smith is a freelance writer, editor, and author. He has covered a wide variety of subjects—including sports, entertainment and travel—for newspapers, magazines, and websites. He has written a nonfiction book about the Washington Nationals and a children's book about Bryce Harper. He lives in the Washington, D.C., area with his wife and two children.